Having Fun with TEXTILES

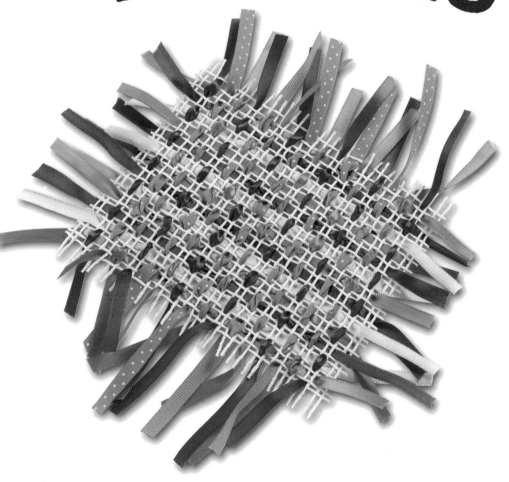

Sarah Medina

WAYLAND

First published in 2007 by Wayland
This paperback edition published in 2009
Copyright © Wayland 2007

Wayland
338 Euston Road
London NW1 3BH

Wayland Australia
Level 17/207 Kent Street
Sydney NSW 2000

Medina, Sarah
  Having fun with textiles. – (Let's do art)
  1. Textile crafts – Juvenile literature
  I. Title
  746

Written by Sarah Medina
Produced by Calcium
Design and model making by Emma DeBanks
Photography by Tudor Photography
Consultancy and concepts by Lisa Regan

ISBN 978-0-7502-5963-7

Printed in China

Wayland is a division of Hachette Children's Books,
an Hachette UK company. www.hachette.co.uk

Contents

Fun with Textiles!

Textiles are the materials we use for clothing, furniture, floors and toys. The projects in this book use different types of textiles. This is what you will need:

- 8-count Aida (special cross-stitch material)
- Felt
- Lace
- Ribbon
- Scraps of material
- Tapestry fabric
- Wool

Note for adults
Children may need adult assistance with some of the project steps. Turn to page 23 for Further Ideas.

Read the 'You will need' boxes carefully for a full list of what you need to make each project.

Before you start, ask an adult to:

- find a surface where you can make the projects.

- find an apron to cover your clothes, or some old clothes that can get messy.

- do things, such as cutting with scissors, that are a little tricky to do on your own.

Groovy Shoes!

Make your shoes groovy with this fun and easy project!

1 Draw big stars and little stars on pieces of felt.

2 Cut out the stars from the felt.

6

3 Fold each star in half and make two slits in the centre, big enough to thread the laces through.

4 Thread the laces through the slits in the stars so the stars are in the middle of the laces.

5 Lace up your shoes with your groovy laces!

 Ask an adult to help you when cutting felt!

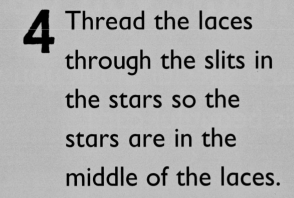

Thank You Card

Say a special thank you with this beautiful card.

1 Cut out one large rectangle of card and one smaller rectangle, and glue the small one to the large one.

2 Using a hole punch, punch six holes on each edge of the larger card.

3 Thread ribbon or lace in and out of all the holes.

4 Tie the ends of the ribbon or lace together in a bow.

5 Now draw a picture or write a thank you note on your card!

 Ask an adult to help you when cutting paper!

Woven Mat

Make a beautiful woven mat that you can put things on!

You will need

- Large-holed tapestry fabric
- Colourful ribbons
- Scissors

1 Cut out a square from the tapestry fabric.

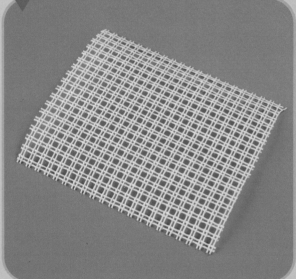

 Ask an adult to help you when cutting fabric!

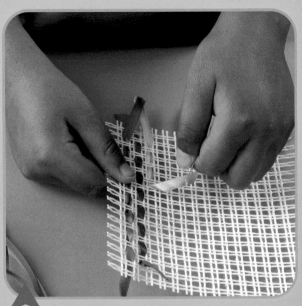

3 Carry on weaving until all the rows have ribbons in place.

2 Starting at one edge, weave one ribbon up through one hole. Leave one hole empty and then weave the ribbon down through the next hole. Repeat to the end of the row.

4 Now weave in the opposite direction, up and down through the holes.

5 Leave the ends loose to form tassels.

Dotty T-Shirt

Have a go at designing your own T-shirt!

You will need
- Plain white T-shirt
- Newspaper
- I sheet of paper
- Black felt-tip pen
- Fabric paints
- Bottle corks

1 Place several sheets of newspaper inside your T-shirt to stop the paint going through to the other side.

2 Draw a design for your T-shirt on paper, and put the paper face up inside the T-shirt and on top of the newspaper.

4 Now print dots around the edge of the sleeves of your T-shirt.

5 Hang your T-shirt up to dry.

3 Dip the end of a cork into fabric paint and print your design onto your T-shirt.

Fridge Magnet

Make a magnetic frame for your favourite photo!

1 Cut out a piece of felt that is bigger than your photo. Cut a rectangle in the middle of the felt so that your photo shows through.

2 Cut out felt shapes and use fabric glue to stick them onto the felt frame.

5 Glue magnets onto the back of the card.

3 Cut a piece of card the same size as the frame and use PVA glue to stick your photo in the middle.

4 Glue the frame onto the front of the card. Make sure you can see your photo!

! Ask an adult to help you when cutting paper/felt!

Stitched Bookmark

Never lose your page again with this bright bookmark!

You will need
- 8cm x 20cm piece of 8-count Aida (cross-stitch material)
- Large darning needle with blunt end
- Long lengths of wool in 5 colours

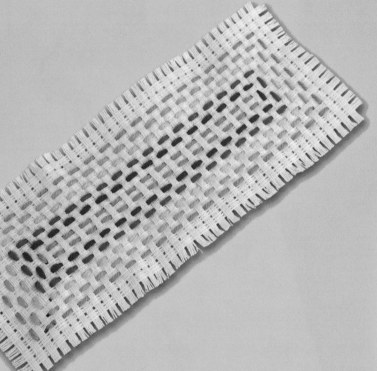

1 Thread your needle with wool and tie a knot in the end.

2 Start stitching three holes down and three holes in. Push your needle up through the first hole and down through the next.

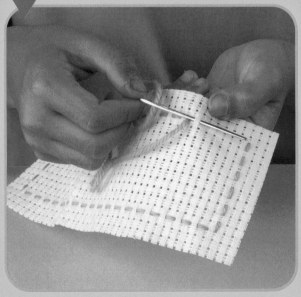

3 Keep stitching all the way round, then tie a knot in the wool close to the back of the material.

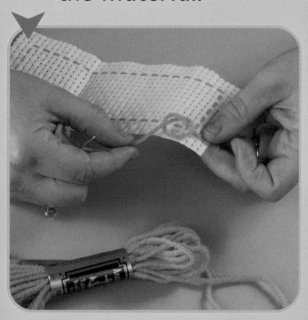

4 Repeat lines of stitching six more times, leaving two squares between each line.

5 Pull away a few strands at each edge to form a fringe.

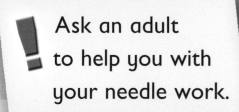

! Ask an adult to help you with your needle work.

Cat Hand Puppet

Play make-believe with this furry friend!

1 Draw a circle onto a piece of felt and cut it out to make a cat's face.

4 Fold each pipe cleaner in half and glue onto the cat to make whiskers.

2 Draw shapes for ears onto felt, cut them out and glue them onto the cat.

3 Glue two beads onto the cat to make eyes. Then glue on another bead to make a nose.

5 Glue your cat onto the front of your glove or mitten.

 Ask an adult to help you when cutting felt!

19

A Beautiful Scene

Enjoy making a lovely
nature scene with all sorts
of different materials!

You will need

- Scraps of fabric in
  different colours
  and textures
- Cotton wool balls
- 1 sheet of card
- Fabric glue
- Scissors

1 Choose a piece of
fabric for the sky
and glue it onto
the card.

2 Cut out some
mountains or hills
from another piece
of fabric and glue
them into place.

3 Choose a colour for the field, cut it out and glue it just beneath the hills and mountains.

4 Cut out a sun and glue it onto the sky.

5 Open out the cotton wool balls a little bit, and glue them onto the sky for clouds.

 Ask an adult to help you when cutting material!

6 Break up a cotton wool ball into small pieces, and glue the pieces onto the picture to make sheep.

7 Cut some flowers out of material and glue them onto your beautiful scene!